Trees

Rachel Bladon

Contents

OXFORD
UNIVERSITY PRESS

D0309033

OXFORD
UNIVERSITY PRESS

Great Clarendon Street, Oxford, OX2 6DP, United Kingdom

Oxford University Press is a department of the University of Oxford. It furthers the University's objective of excellence in research, scholarship, and education by publishing worldwide. Oxford is a registered trade mark of Oxford University Press in the UK and in certain other countries

ISBN: 978 0 19 464636 9

An Audio CD Pack containing this book and a CD is also available, ISBN 978 0 19 464646 8

The CD has a choice of American and British English recordings of the complete text.

An accompanying Activity Book is also available, ISBN 978 0 19 464657 4

Printed in China

This book is printed on paper from certified and well-managed sources.

ACKNOWLEDGEMENTS

Illustrations by:

Kelly Kennedy pp.5, 6, 7, 11, 17; Alan Rowe pp.20, 22, 23, 25, 26, 27, 30, 31.

The Publishers would also like to thank the following for their kind permission to reproduce photographs and other copyright material: Alamy pp.3 (snowy conifers/ FB-Fischer/imagebroker), 5 (Chris Pearsall), 11 (David Entrican), 15 (log cabin/Directphoto.org, totem pole/T. Schaeffer/Arco Images GmbH); Getty Images pp.3 (tree in park/Andrew Watson/Photolibrary), 7 (Arunas Klupsas/Photolibrary), 14 (car/William West/AFP), 19 (logging/Danita Delimont/Gallo Images); Naturepl.com pp.16 (Andy Rouse), 17 (snake/Daniel Heuclin), 18 (Andy Rouse); Oxford University Press pp.3 (apple tree, tree on beach), 4, 6, 9 (apple tree/cut apple), 10 (broadleaves/conifers), 12, 13, 14 (fruit market), 17 (monkey), 19 (tree planting); Science Photo Library p.8 (David R. Frazier Photolibrary, Inc.).

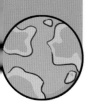

Introduction

Trees are all around us, in forests, gardens, and parks. There are many different trees, and they give us many things.

Where do you see trees?
What do we get from trees?

Now read and discover more about trees!

What Is a Tree?

A tree is a tall plant. It has leaves, branches, a trunk, and roots.

A Tree

leaves

branch

trunk

roots

A tree makes its food with light from the sun. It grows tall so it can get lots of light.

 Discover!

Some coast redwood trees are 110 meters tall!

A tree grows every day. Look at this old tree trunk. How old is it? Count the rings. Every ring is one year.

An Old Tree Trunk

ring

Go to page 20 for activities.

Parts of a Tree

What do the different parts of a tree do?

Leaves grow on branches. They make food for the tree. To make food they use water, air, and light from the sun.

leaves

sun

air

light

water

Roots take water from the ground.

The trunk takes food down the tree from the leaves, and it takes water up the tree from the roots.

Bark is the wood on the outside of the trunk. It protects the trunk.

Go to page 21 for activities.

Flowers and Seeds

Some trees have big flowers. Some trees have very little flowers.

Flowers make pollen. The wind blows pollen from one flower to other flowers. Insects take pollen to other flowers, too. Then the tree can grow seeds.

flower

pollen

seed

Fruit on a Tree

Seeds grow inside fruit. The fruit protects the seeds. The fruit falls from the tree. Then the seeds go into the ground. New trees grow from the seeds!

→ Go to page 22 for activities.

 Different Trees

Some trees are broadleaves, and some trees are conifers. Broadleaves have flat leaves. Conifers have thin, sharp needles.

Conifers are strong trees. Animals can't eat the sharp needles. The needles don't get dry so the trees can grow in dry weather. Conifers can grow in hot weather or cold weather.

Broadleaves

leaves

Conifers

needles

In Cold Weather

In Hot Weather

Many broadleaves can't grow in cold weather or dry weather. Then all the leaves fall off the tree. The leaves grow again in hot weather or rainy weather.

Half a million leaves can fall off a very, very big tree!

→ Go to page 23 for activities.

What Trees Do

Trees are good for us! We use oxygen in the air to live. Too much carbon dioxide in the air is bad for us. Trees clean the air. They take carbon dioxide out of the air, and they put oxygen into the air.

carbon dioxide

oxygen

Trees protect us from the rain and the light from the sun.

Trees are good for the ground, too. The roots make the ground strong. The ground around trees isn't dry, so other plants can grow.

We can play and have fun in trees, too! Thank you, trees!

→ Go to page 24 for activities.

6 Things from Trees

Fruit

Apples, oranges, bananas, nuts, and lots of other fruit grow on trees.

We get rubber from trees, too. We make car tires and many other things with rubber.

A Car with Rubber Tires

tire

Wood in a Home

The trunks and branches of trees give us wood. We make toys, tables, homes, and many other things with wood. We make paper with wood. We use wood to make fires, too.

Discover!

In North America, there are amazing totem poles. People make them from trees!

Go to page 25 for activities.

Many birds, insects, and other animals live in trees. Animals can find food there. Trees protect animals from the wind and rain. Trees can protect animals from other animals, too.

This monkey lives in a tree. It eats leaves and fruit from the tree. It can move from branch to branch.

A Monkey

This snake lives in a tree, too. It likes its home. It can find birds to eat there. Foxes and other big animals can't catch the snake in the tree.

A Snake

Discover!

Some plants live in trees, too!

Go to page 26 for activities.

Some animals and little plants are bad for trees. Animals eat the leaves and bark. Little plants grow around the trunk. Then the tree can't get water.

People are bad for trees, too. Cars, fires, and factories can make the air and rain dirty. Then the trees can't grow.

Some people cut down trees. They take wood and they make new things on the land.

Every day people cut down about 10 million trees.

Let's stop this. Let's grow new trees. Let's protect trees!

Go to page 27 for activities.

1 What Is a Tree?

← Read pages 4–5.

1 Write the words.

branches   leaves
trunk   roots

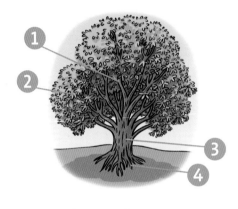

1   _branches_

2   _____

3   _____

4   _____

2 Complete the sentences.

food   light   branches   year   plant

1 A tree is a tall ___plant___ .

2 A tree has leaves, _____ , a trunk, and roots.

3 A tree makes its _____ with light from the sun.

4 A tree grows tall so it can get _____ .

5 On a tree trunk, every ring is one _____ .

2 Parts of a Tree

← Read pages 6–7.

1 Match.

1 Leaves
2 Roots
3 The trunk
4 Bark

take water from the ground.
takes food down the tree and water up the tree.
make food for the tree.
protects the trunk.

2 Circle the correct words.

1 Leaves grow on (branches) / bark.

2 Bark **makes** / **protects** the trunk.

3 To make food for the tree, leaves use water, **air** / **roots**, and light from the sun.

4 Bark is the wood on the outside of the **trunk** / **leaf**.

5 Leaves, **roots,** / **light**, the trunk, and bark are parts of a tree.

3 Flowers and Seeds

← Read pages 8–9.

1 Complete the sentences.

> wind   pollen   Flowers   big

1   Some trees have_____ flowers.

2   _____ on trees make pollen.

3   The _____ blows pollen from one
flower to other flowers.

4   Insects take _____ to other flowers.

2 Number the sentences in order. Then number the pictures.

☐   The fruit falls from the tree.

☐   The seeds go in the ground.

☐   New trees grow.

1   Seeds grow inside fruit.

④ Different Trees

← Read pages 10–11.

1 Complete the puzzle.

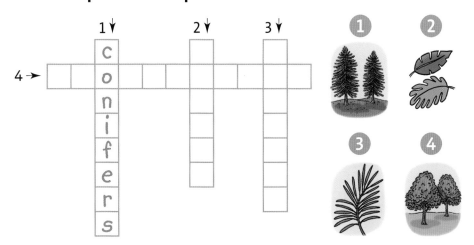

2 Write *true* or *false*.

1 Conifers have flat leaves. _false_

2 Broadleaves have thin, sharp needles. _____

3 Animals can eat the sharp needles on conifers. _____

4 Many broadleaves can't grow in cold weather. _____

5 Half a million leaves can fall off a very, very big tree. _____

5 What Trees Do

← Read pages 12–13.

1 Circle the correct words.

1 We use oxygen in the air to **live** / **eat**.

2 Too much **oxygen** / **carbon dioxide** in the air is bad for us.

3 Trees are **good** / **bad** for the ground.

4 Tree roots make the **air** / **ground** strong.

5 The **ground** / **wind** around trees doesn't dry out.

2 Complete the sentences.

rain   sun   clean   play
oxygen   carbon dioxide

1 Trees _____ the air.

2 Trees take _____ out of the air.

3 Trees put _____ into the air.

4 Trees protect us from the _____ and the light from the _____ .

5 We can _____ and have fun in trees.

6 Things from Trees

← Read pages 14–15.

1 Find and write the words.

r	w	o	o	d	a
r	u	b	b	e	r
b	a	n	p	e	a
b	p	a	p	e	r
e	s	t	e	y	p
f	r	u	i	t	i
e	s	n	r	o	a

1   _rubber_

2   w _____

4   f _____

3   p _____

2 Answer the questions.

1 What do we make with rubber?

   We make car tires and many other
   things with rubber.

2 What parts of a tree give us wood?

   _____

3 What do we make with wood?

   _____

7 Homes in Trees

← Read pages 16–17.

1 Write the words.

> snake   insects
> bird   monkey

 1 _____

 2 _____

 3 _____

 4 _____

2 Order the words.

1 trees. / animals / in / Many / live

　Many animals live in trees.

2 trees. / can / in / Animals / food / find

_____

3 monkey / leaves / The / fruit. / eats / and

_____

4 lives / tree. / The / a / snake / in

_____

8 Protect Trees!

← Read pages 18–19.

1 Match. Then write the numbers.

1 People	grow around tree trunks.
2 Little plants	cut down trees.
3 Animals	eat tree leaves and bark.

2 Answer the questions.

1 What things are bad for trees?

_____

2 What makes the air and rain dirty?

_____

3 How many trees do people cut down every day?

_____

Project · Trees Where I Live

1 Find two trees near where you live.
Complete the charts.

Tree 1

1 Does it have ...   leaves? ☐   needles? ☐

2 Is it ...   a broadleaf? ☐   a conifer? ☐

3 Does it have ...

   flowers? ☐   leaves? ☐   fruit? ☐

4 In the tree, can you see ...

   other plants? ☐   animals? ☐

Tree 2

1 Does it have ...   leaves? ☐   needles? ☐

2 Is it ...   a broadleaf? ☐   a conifer? ☐

3 Does it have ...

   flowers? ☐   leaves? ☐   fruit? ☐

4 In the tree, can you see ...

   other plants? ☐   animals? ☐

2 Draw pictures of the trees. Then write the words.

Tree 1	Tree 2

leaves / needles
flowers / fruit

leaves / needles
flowers / fruit

3 Write sentences about the trees.

Tree 1 _____

_____

_____

Tree 2 _____

_____

_____

Picture Dictionary

air

animals

blow

clean

cut down

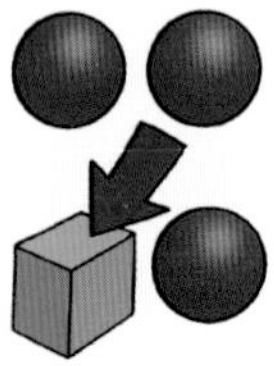

different

dirty

down

dry

factory

fall

fire

flat

food

forest

fruit

 ground

 grow

 half

 insects

 land

 leaves

 light

 million

 plants

 pollen

 protect

 seeds

 sharp

 strong

 up

wood

Oxford Read and Discover

Series Editor: Hazel Geatches • CLIL Adviser: John Clegg

Oxford Read and Discover graded readers are at six levels, for students from age 6 and older. They cover many topics within three subject areas, and support English across the curriculum, or Content and Language Integrated Learning (CLIL).

Available for each reader:
- Audio Pack
- Activity Book

Available for selected readers:
- e-Books

Teaching notes & CLIL guidance: **www.oup.com/elt/teacher/readanddiscover**

Subject Area / Level	The World of Science & Technology	The Natural World	The World of Arts & Social Studies
1 300 headwords	• Eyes • Fruit • Trees • Wheels	• At the Beach • In the Sky • Wild Cats • Young Animals	• Art • Schools
2 450 headwords	• Electricity • Plastic • Sunny and Rainy • Your Body	• Camouflage • Earth • Farms • In the Mountains	• Cities • Jobs
3 600 headwords	• How We Make Products • Sound and Music • Super Structures • Your Five Senses	• Amazing Minibeasts • Animals in the Air • Life in Rainforests • Wonderful Water	• Festivals Around the World • Free Time Around the World
4 750 headwords	• All About Plants • How to Stay Healthy • Machines Then and Now • Why We Recycle	• All About Desert Life • All About Ocean Life • Animals at Night • Incredible Earth	• Animals in Art • Wonders of the Past
5 900 headwords	• Materials to Products • Medicine Then and Now • Transportation Then and Now • Wild Weather	• All About Islands • Animal Life Cycles • Exploring Our World • Great Migrations	• Homes Around the World • Our World in Art
6 1,050 headwords	• Cells and Microbes • Clothes Then and Now • Incredible Energy • Your Amazing Body	• All About Space • Caring for Our Planet • Earth Then and Now • Wonderful Ecosystems	• Food Around the World • Helping Around the World